SHEDDING THE NICETIES

Also by Ellen Phethean

POETRY

Sauce, The Poetry Virgins (Bloodaxe Books, 1994)
Wall (Smokestack Books, 2007)
Breath (Flambard, 2009. Reprinted Red Squirrel Press, 2014)
Portrait of the Quince as an Older Woman (Red Squirrel Press, 2014)
Women Talking (self-published, 2020)

FICTION

YA trilogy
Ren and the Blue Hands (Postbox Press, 2016)
Ren and the Blue Cloth (Postbox Press, 2019)
Ren in Samara (Postbox Press, 2019)

For Sam

SHEDDING THE NICETIES

Best Wishes
Ellen Phethean

ELLEN PHETHEAN

RED SQUIRREL PRESS

First published in 2023 by Red Squirrel Press
36 Elphinstone Crescent
Biggar
South Lanarkshire
ML12 6GU
www.redsquirrelpress.com

Layout, design and typesetting by Gerry Cambridge
gerry.cambridge@btinternet.com

A CIP catalogue record for this book is available from
the British Library.

ISBN: 978 1 913632 44 1

Red Squirrel Press is committed to a sustainable future.
This publication is printed in the UK by Imprint Digital using
Forest Stewardship Council certificated paper.
www.digital.imprint.co.uk

Contents

For all the women in my life—friends and family—
with love and thanks

My Source Inside

My vowel sounds are sanctioned by the south:
I offer words like damaged goods,
fear they'll be amusing or misunderstood.
From finis terre to end of Englishness,
traverse the geography of time and life.
Upend the map, make the jigsaw fit
a different way, unsettle home. Like roots
uprooted, edges are inheritance—

the Tyne a frontier on my skin, the wind, the craic,
the singing tongue familiar-foreign—

North.

Cuckmere Haven

In reach of London in the Austin,
the weekend scent of leather seats,
tartan rug, sliced bread and fish paste,
fug of cigarettes, and travel sweets.
Stops for petrol, nappies, car sick,
arguments about the route, family spats—
who sits front or back. To keep
the peace a threat of Father's smack.

A post-war pillbox, chalky cliffs
and shingle frame the scene:
Tom's knee-length shorts and schoolboy fringe
all buckled-up in gabardine;
teenage Jean in outgrown sun dress,
awkward in her ankle socks,
and little Nutmeg, grumpy, rocks
the baby in the Moses basket.

Father in a pea coat, fag in hand
and Mother, humming *Don't Fence Me In,*
shares out food; getting away
from carpets, dust and cooking, being
outdoors, her element—a nomad
in a former life, survivor—
she would have kept on travelling.
But Father was the driver.

The Texture of Memory

Lying under the green counterpane
the dark expands
air slowly disappears
silence stifles breath:
is she emptying out
or is the room filling her?

Trees rhythmic, agitated,
move against yellow curtains,
faint and far away, trains
rumble, calling to the night: the world

outside the room is uncontainable, yet here
inside her head.
Is she tiny or immense?

Girl

is a waiting room, her body awkward
luggage,

the moon's her companion,
an eye which closes and opens
very slowly.

Her thoughts
shuffling and grabbing:

trials are part of it
as her life sings its becoming—
dancing bones, blood chuckling,

the chalky scrape
of nails and hair inching out,

the elastane of curves,
her skin a slim sheaf
about to be written.

Sanitary Arrangements

One pair of knickers, rust-stained
a drawer in the family chest on the landing (not for the use of boys)
belt (passed on from sisters) losing elasticity
a bag of thick cotton pads, with loops
a rolled up swimming costume and towel, unused
loose-fitting, wide-legged hessian trousers, purple, hand-made
a darkened room, an old sofa
2 aspirin and a glass of water
Moonfleet: an abandoned book
the smell of iron, something on the turn

The Dark Side

I trailed along the High Street
in clingy cheesecloth shirt,
a mini-skirt and flip-flops,
to an old green pub, worn-out men
permanently poised on leather stools,
flatulent and grumbling. I swatted
banter, wiping glasses, fumbling change,
a floor show for these dimming lives.

Lacking light
I had to lean in close
to read the lips, work out ales,
raise my arms behind the bar,
pump in one hand, pint in the other,
had to stand on the dark side
where the landlord's hand
found my bare thighs.

As I sat beside his wife on the chintz
to collect my first and last pay packet,
hazed in smoke
with spectacles and lapdog,
she asked me: Is it him?
No, I said, of course not, no.

Polly

Pretty and vulnerable,
often dead precocious; abandoned in
Lordship Lane, a house full of brothers, red
lips she practised pouting.
Years when we wanted to be the other. She
liked my cheekbones, I loved her cheek.
Us together, laughing, swigging. Who really
cared? I went north, she went to
AA.
Show me how it could have gone differently.

Shuggy Boat Gigolo

Her lips meet his on the upward swing
of the sauce boat. She wears no ring,
he stands, wide trousers, waspy waist,
pinning her to the moment, all muscle and poise.
With carefree arms and brylcreemed hair, he's done it
hundreds of times before; her hand grips
the pole. Is it fresh air—would she have succumbed
with her feet on the ground, or has she been waiting for this,
her best, or is it her only, real kiss?
From Hoppings to Lammas Fair, what's the draw,
the dangerous urge to fly? Perhaps it's like war:
we let our defences down—the rules relax
for the nearness of death—the chance of sex
or loss thrusting us into that first embrace.

The Ring I Never Wore

wasn't part of our language—
soft rain, friendly pubs, northern
vowels; a new tongue,
unrecognisable mouth
shaping questions
parents didn't understand.

We chose other 'rings':
chairs in a workshop,
a silver mouthpiece,
camera aperture, megaphone,
circles round a fire.

What does my naked finger do now?
Like a light-house
it works automatically
speaking to the dark sea

on which it draws
a ring of summer gold.

Le Poète Allongé

painting by Marc Chagall

Why me ? I am a tired poet lying on damp grass.
I cannot make the sun set.
There's no logic in it. I could have been a dancer.
I sense the violet sky: it's getting cold, I'll have to put my coat on.
The horse eats, the pig grunts, evening will come, this is their world.
A poet asks questions because the world wants answers.
Why me ? Only death is a certainty: I recline.

Poet in Pieces on the Roscommon Road

It's not Ireland but it is.
You cycle along with one leg
and no poems. It's all going horribly wrong.
Heaney and parrot will both be there.
Kavanagh's trilby is waving you on:
Will you be coming at all? he calls.
Three cows are waiting:
The Poetry Lovers.
Arseholed, smashed,
you can't remember your name,
eyes splinter, nose drips,
face splits into jagged halves.
Your man from the Catholic Times
takes the picture. You have your title and first line.

The Trick

I have decided to read poems
as if they are all addressed to me
personally
by a therapist
or a palm reader.

Darkening a Dress

Rain, shadow, blood—all darken fabric,
patterns overlaid on the hung-out dress
reminder of summer and conquest,
its empty weight a betrayal,
a shape remembering a body.
A rose blooms on its half-heartedness.
It hangs helpless, bothered by the wind
and ghosts who tug, wanting substance.

Rosebay Willowherb

loves the dangerous rush of trains,
doesn't understand gardens or fences,
laughs at strimmers, prim borders,
prefers being on the brink, upsetting order.
Needs space, to feel wind lift her rags,
she inherits the wild and secret places,
haunt of foragers and trespassers.

Named for her pink face, her tag
is Fireweed. She's spiky, strong,
brings life to the abandoned, bombed
and dispossessed.
Proof of power in numbers,
she goes on and on.
You can't kill the spirit.

Love Conkers

We kick through papery leaves for the green mines
waiting to explode, mottled spiky skin
reptilian and foreign; inside, rich mahogany
of a Jag dashboard, or the parlour table.

The licensed violence of conquer season, the mashed limbs
of sticks sent flying to bring down the fruit,
boys string them up as weapons, smashed to victory.
Girls gather them like rare gems—

how they shrivel, lose their lustre so soon
gather dust and we wonder what
all the fuss was about; but we loved them
for their short afternoon.

Silva

Slowly we grow   we know   about Time

       Winds blow   snow passes   aeons

return   and go

              when you think us dead   or dormant   oh no

we lie low   we know   how to wait   with patience

       we sow   our seeds

          we show green   buds

embroider berries on mossy cloth

            our children lie beneath

       we put them   to bed

               we have many under our skin
we keep their secret

Closer to Humans than Plants

Under the trees in the park
amongst the green bushes,
there's a fruiting body,

stem rising from the loam
exposing itself:
paraphilia toadstool.

Growing in the dark
it's been waiting
for the right conditions.

Pink, silky cap,
frill of gills, milk bell,
cleft lip, slit-eyed

snake, spores
fine as smoke—
once shed, it collapses.

In their kingdom of mould and smuts,
they thrive on living tissue.
Ancient lore tells us they grow

where witches meet.

Semana Santa

In fading coral sky a moon grows;
      winding away from the Alhambra
           comes the statue of The Lady
     carried on a dining table draped in white,
below, a sea of trainers
     edging down the road
           behind a band of buglers who blow
    Moorish high notes, bent
beyond a western scale,
     weird and luminous.

        Every twenty yards or so
    the structure falters, feet stop,
tobacco smoke billows
     from underneath the rood,
          holy,
    alien to us,
hot in sandals,
     loose silk shirts,
       who amble
           enchanted,
    anticipating beers, our cool room.

Union

You arrived, an idea in a knitted hat and mittens
packed in a box on the kitchen table.

We forgot about you and were startled
by your cry, wrecking our schedule,

testing our *laissez-faire* arrangements,
demanding hands-on improvisation

with night feeds, nappies, holding, rocking,
pushing, undressing, washing, a factory line

of endless needs. You were Foreman,
we the tired labourers who struggled

against the shocking hours and work conditions
as we watched the clock for the end of the shift

that never came.
But you paid us in love and we became rich.

Son

A blue whale a thousand miles away,
his underwater song reaches across the deep.

Unexpected, he crashes up through the water
surfacing, throwing my balance,

larger than life, magnificent,
reckless.

Sleek and undeniable, hunting for something
he flops down, makes waves,

then he's gone.

I might not see him again for months,
but I long for that glimpse—

both of us solitary mammals,
warm blooded, we breathe the same air.

The Southbound Platform

echoes with advice
and information that we cannot grasp
unlike our bags on wheels held close and filled
with all we need to journey—night things, tooth
brush, underwear. Our paper bought and stuffed
into the zip-up pocket, coffee carton
clutched, we check our watches, phones, the screen,
we hear the yellow numbers click away.
Some touch or talk, we look to find the spot
that's ours, marked A to K: we stand, heads turned
and scan the silver rails in the sun.
We're in the shade, anticipate the thrum
of diesel, the slow heave and smell of oil,
while out beyond the brick and iron archway
lies the future, and the past, that we're
not part of now but here in the eternal
present, fingering our tickets.

When We Drank From Streams

and ate with our fingers,
wrapping food in leaves,
we had no need of washing up.

My mother showed me how spoons
could be scoured with clods of earth,
wiped on the grass, dipped in pools.

You and I had a red plastic bowl,
a drying rack balancing glass,
pans and dangerous knives.
I needed rubber gloves to protect my skin.

Your brother had a modern kitchen,
a dishwasher he loaded in a particular way,
cleaning the crocks before
he put them in.

You didn't want one, liking your fingers
in a warm place in our draughty house.
It gave you space to think.

Then you were gone
and I had to do it all. Be careful
what you wish for.

Now I recycle the same cup and plate,
eat with my fingers,
drink straight from the tap.

Five O'Clock Shadow

He cursed it,
sometimes let it grow—
beard chic
to homeless stubble
within a space of days—
only ever using water, soap, steel
leaving flecks of blood,
bits of tissue stuck to his chin,
as if something inside had been exposed,
his face tender, raw
flayed
like the last time I saw him.

Poem in Which I Bring Back the Dead

Names have power. I breathe his,
revive its vowels and consonants.
I wear his thick socks, he's keeping me warm—
pluck his guitar and whistle his tunes
so he can be heard all over the house.
Letters arrive addressed to him—
he's alive on somebody's list.
He's in another country drinking wine:
I recognise that out-of-season hotel—
the mist around him, how it all grows faint
at the border where travellers meet or miss—
I'll bring my passport, his watch, and wait.

Today

All over the city,
people are getting ready:
hunting out clean socks,

standing shoeless
ironing a good frock,
struggling to knot the blasted tie,

touching a pocket for the words,
not touching the toast,
looking over the list again.

Opening the front door,
checking the weather,
tapping their feet, waiting for taxis.

Giving a hand to guide
the old, the young.
Stepping out, locking up.

All over the city
streets will become unfamiliar
this last day, the first.

Coming to Terms with Spring

Once, I ached and raged
against clueless snowdrops,
felt sun cut like a knife, halving my room.
Warm air laughed, daffodils trumpeted
about nothing, mud obscured my way,
bare trees, loitering, stared me out.
What was Spring to me?
I looked backwards, into earth,
sharp green shoots pierced my heart.

This morning the rain on my window
said Spring had retreated.
I sat in darkness, a cup of tea
in bed, listening to the recycling lorry
smashing glass in the back lane.
I got up and showered,
dressed in green and purple,
put on my gold oak-leaf earrings
and noticed my hair was growing.

Nature Morte

As children's voices drift in
through the open window
that old woman in the mirror shocks her.
No-one to reach the awkward zip
or share the pot of Assam in the morning.
Remembering her lost ones,
slipping into the bardo seeking news
from the other side
of how this will go,
her life is play-acting and
over the horizon is dark.
I am in mourning for my life.
She wants to be touched
by someone other than a nurse.

No.
She will be unruly,
throw off her mask, inhabit herself,
open up to the life, till now,
she was dreaming,
go naked into the Tyne at dusk,
swim into deep water.
She knows
she must cross
the reeking world
of tide line, between high and low,
where the lost and the travelled
come to rest, half-buried in silt,
to reach the sharp cold river
that will slap her
into consciousness
like a midwife.

Grenfell

The communication
of the dead is tongued with fire—T. S. Eliot

The tribe in white with tip
-toe tread invade
the reeking tower with
tweezer, trowel and tub
and pay minute attention
to their job.
Like mythic ants,
on bended knees they sift
each blackened relic:
tooth or cloth or bone?
With sieve and plastic
packet, pick
through evidence of life,
the little clues,
remains of ashy puzzles.
Resealing rooms, and ticking
lists, they leave.
What care, what cash,
what lengthy months for this,
at last, a close inspection.
While those whose lives
were saved or spent,
lie waiting in the dark.

Frida Kahlo's Eyebrow Pencil in the V&A

Bright lights bring me back from the dark
to the high society of her dressing table:
red lipsticks speak her name,
silk scarves, parrot seed,
silver earrings will peck her chin,
the morning cut of crimson
bougainvillea blooms to hook behind her ears.
Her skin and prints mark me, I'm her thing—
I await our tryst with mirror, our ritual
of look, lean in, and glide,
a line of distant hills, outspread eagle's wings,
her lovely brow.

I lie, I wait, I sigh.
She's not coming, I know that now.

Joy

She stands before the mirror clothed in milky light
marvelling at her nakedness. Mother offers
a camisole of pale blewitt with lilac trim
and attends to her daughter's hair with an ivory brush.
They sing in harmony All things bright and beautiful.

As the elder fastens tiny mother-of-pearl buttons
smoothing out the satin gown, the younger
whispers I have the shivers.
Natural my dear, says the matron, Here's a posset of dittany
to calm you.
Finally, Mother sets a white floret upon her daughter's head
and both weep at the sight in the mirror, holding hands and smiling.

The Poet and Potter's Affair

She communicates with him every day

sitting in her bed,

letters, scrabble-like, spelling out

their long distance game—

while Kiss and Come can be

squeezed in (with luck

the Kiss starting on a triple)

Love is awkward, there are no

two letter words to be made

with a V, and C can only

couple with H—he charmed her with

Haiku, she replied with Raku.

It's the luck

of the draw: using all her tiles

she got a high score

with Unrequited.

Mother Painting Godolphin woods

The bluebell's glamour
steals the power of speech,

her tired heart floats
through rings of memory

to an unreachable place
of hand and eye

strung between past and future
where she's lost to us—

she's a lone dog hunting
the shadowy garlic

sniffing out the hidden
connectedness of things.

Father in the High Bed

Blueish skin papery thin,
stretched tight on bones,
body curled in, like his mind.

I roused him with *Dad?*
At my voice, his eyelids slid up,
revealed black wells;

though he couldn't speak
I'd made my last connection
on his journey down,

the hard relinquishing,
a slow dwindle to newborn,
ready for the cradle of fire.

Journey's End

I travel with his old haversack,
army khaki, lots of pockets

holding the phrase book
where is the station/toilet/hotel, please, thank you;

dark glasses for the glare; sunscreen;
map, dog-eared and frayed

at the corners, that he annotated
with mileage; campsites circled in green

down the coast of Yugoslavia,
a name that no longer exists

like the campfire, guy ropes,
the scent of hot canvas.

The purse: jade, pink, and tasselled,
not easily mislaid, for my Euros,

unlike the zlotys, lira and drachma
he kept in an envelope tucked in the bookcase.

The taverna still blooms
with bougainvillea and clematis.

Retracing his steps, history erased, borders redrawn,
I will return empty-handed, lighter.

The Invisible Woman

Une femme d'un certain age,
they take my tongue, my face,
my name fades from their list,
no-one remembers my books,
I'm transparent,
an empty space
their eyes glide over.

They take my finery: two pearl earrings,
a Jay's feather quill, my silk scarf;
I put on the anorak of dusk.
As I walk the street
their catcalls and applause
do not follow me,
the words of fathers ringing in my ears
a man
is like fine wine, he improves with age,
for us it's a sin: we're their terrible mirror
who speaks.

Do they suppose I have a cupboard
in which I lock my passions?
That my portion is adequate:
pain perdu, a glass of rosé?

Women with nothing to lose
who laugh, at ease, share my space.
We see each other,
discuss our work: a History of Invisible Women.

Do they suppose we are patient?

The Song of the Cockroach

You may mock—
let me tell you
my head's bent to see my path
and mouth's awkward
for it's hard to keep smiling,
I don't bite, but folk avoid me.
Limbs rough from work,
clinging to existence;
nights spent between kitchen,
bathroom, laundry, hot and humid.
I've been around. Done my time
in the underside of others' homes.
I know a thing or two about dirt.

I like the summer months, hate the smell of lime,
and have a sweet tooth.
A louche sisterhood, we rub along fine.
No-one wants to touch us.
It might come as a shock
but we were bright nymphs in our youth,
we've seen the morning of the world.
So don't reproach me;
I come from an ancient line,
I may be old, back brittle, voice cracked,
but I can survive (unlike you)
atomic winter.

Cullercoats Cows

Just before sunrise,
horizon tipped with ice and fire

shivering on the gritty sand,
black costume, rubber shoes,

bobble hat hugging her head,
jostling the other old seals

cackling and groaning misty puffs
into the half-dark, she advances

to the waves, wades in,
cold tightening wrinkled skin,

plunges, short of breath,
shock leaving her speechless.

Grace shows her death,
lets her live another day.

Northern Echo

Bellowing down the Pennine Way,
it thunders over the High Force drop

to run between the dales and ricochets
under graffitied bridges, along metro tracks,

it's a boom from a hooter fading to mist,
rattle of cranes and rusted ships,

the lost clank of the pit-head wheel,
the dying fall of the steel worker's whistle,

a hiss of water on hot metal,
a piss in a pot, if there was one to piss in.

Carried on wind that howls and bites,
it mutters about food banks and stolen bikes.

It's the call of a paper seller late at night
in a business park, empty and bright,

or the endless roar of the A1M.
It's someone weeping, shouting a name

down a street to those
who'll not come again.

It Was Never Ours

Margaret taught us that:
national treasures snatched
like little bottles of milk.
Starting with the smallest,
she worked her way up
to grown men, who muscled
underground;
brought them to their knees
in mean streets,
made us weep.

Fighting back
I trespassed,
blowing my trumpet—
the Red Flag.
So what?
my silence says now.
All I own is dust.
Those on the Left prove
the closer you are, the more you hate.

We should speak to the dead—
everything has a story to tell
if we ask the right questions.

Theme Park

It costs to leave
the Gift Shop
that smells of candles,
boudoir soap,
sweet and antiseptic as a hospice.
There's a mug
with your name on
as you're jostled by others
all wanting out.
Each must purchase
a key-ring or puzzle
to appease the gods of Heritage.
There's tea towels
How to Talk Geordie:
wor lass, gan canny.
Ex-miners cough
haway man, it's fifteen poonds!
Proggy mats and baking bread,
the mournful whistle,
safety lamps and back shift,
firedamp, rock fall, emphysema,
working class—

there's no way back.

Arrival, Millennium Bridge

It had to be just right: the weather, wind
and water. Waiting for the day the river,
mirroring the cloudless sky, stood still.

The tide was on the turn, riding up
from Jarrow slakes to Wylam, when the giant
hove into view, wide as the Tyne,

golden yellow against the blue, riveting
in autumn light. Not a breath to tilt
or sway the floating sheerleg crane,

elegant as Nureyev and Fonteyn,
the Asian Hercules lifted, hovered,
swung and lowered the blinking eye

into its slot with millimetre precision.
The crowd were silent till that drop

then how we cheered, as old lads felt the tug,
the thrill, clapped the hands that helped to build
that moment.

Who Knows?

November is when nights darken early—
we walk like ghosts in the gathering twilight
following footpaths to mysterious ends.
Don't say I love you.
Listen for the thunder of faraway trains
or trace the mutter of fast-flowing water.
You are so sedentary, my dear old friend.
Don't ask me the time.
Look up at the dome of sky over us,
can you see the Andromeda Galaxy?
Don't talk about love, nothing is certain
but stars and dark.
Snow is melting, the river is moving on,
let's go home, face the night together.

Afterwards

Don't be floored when I disappear
to a chapel on a moor,
(feral with wind

buffeting pink thrift and gorse,
carrying the smell of sea)
with white walls, a vaulted ceiling

and windows that eat light,
a space I'll portion, like God,
into day and night.

I might practise yoga in the kitchen,
paint in bed, learn to bend yellow and blue
into every shade. No mirrors,

only memory and imagination.
If you find my door and knock,
and if I let you in,

don't be surprised
by my silence.
I'll have shed the niceties.

Auld Acquaintance

I saw the new moon like an eye
too cold to open fully in the inky sky.
The sleety snow fell on my tongue
tasting stale, of the year just gone.
I smelt the whisky on my breath
that clung in droplets to my scarf,
and heard my footsteps echo
in the ice-cave of the park.

When the ground slid off
        I had to grab the bitter metal rail,
thinking I'm a fool to walk alone,
unaided, tipsy, in the dark.

I felt the old familiar pain
grip my heart, then let go again.

Kenneggy

The tree-shaded table and chair
nestle by a Cornish hedge,

heat of late day
warms my back,

honeysuckle's sweetness rises
from a mass of brambles.

The gin and tonic glass icy
to my hand,

a tang of lemon on my tongue,
bubbles in my mouth.

Over the fields to the cliff
the house on the headland's

granite walls sparkle in the rays
of the setting sun.

A blue-as-forget-me-not's sea
is soft as well-washed cotton.

If there's a heaven,
let it be this

like a long breath out

Acknowledgements

'My Source Inside', originally published as 'Exile—821': Northern Poetry
       library website

'Cuckmere Haven': VANE WOMEN—25 years (2016)

'Girl': The High Window magazine Spring 2022

'Sanitary Arrangements': Dreich 5, 2020

'The Ring I Never Wore': Women Talking, some lines inspired by
       R. S. Thomas' autumn diary

'Le Poète Allongé' a painting by Marc Chagall

'Poet in Pieces on the Roscommon Road': The NORTH issue 48
       Oct 2011

'Rosebay Willowherb': One Planet Anthology, Newcastle Uni Alumni
       Day of Action—Poems for the Planet

'Love Conkers': The Iron Book of Tree Poetry, 2020

'Silva': Lovely, Dark and Deep: Poems About Woods, Grey Hen, 2021

'Union': Witches, Warriors, Workers, Culture Matters Co-operative, 2020

'When We Drank From Streams': Dreich 5 2020

'Poem in Which I Bring Back the Dead': Poetry Prescription, Newcastle
       University 2015

'Nature Morte', first published as 'In Two Minds': The High Window
       magazine Spring 2022

'Grenfell' Summer Anywhere, Dreich Anthology 2021

'Joy': Dreich 5 2020

'The Invisible Woman': Women Talking

Thanks to the women's poetry group for support and inspiration.
Thanks to Carte Blanche, where many of these poems began.
With special thanks to Pippa Little for her help and expert eye on
these poems.

A NOTE ON THE TYPES

The main text of this book is set in Seria Pro,
the Dutch type designer Martin Majoor's
'literary' typeface, released in 2000. Seria is a
beautiful serif with a distinctive italic. It is paired
here with the companion sans serif Seria Sans Pro
for titles and occasional other matter.